CHARLES LETTS · FOUNDED 1796 · Letts

LEARNING WITH LETTS

For five- to six-ye olds

Kerry's Cart

Story by Irene Yates
Activities by David Bell, Geoff Leyland,
Mick Seller and Irene Yates

Illustrations by Peter Joyce

People who live in Cherry Walk

For my mum

Gran was nice and early.
'Thought I'd come for breakfast!'
she said when Kerry let her in.

There were kisses all round and
lots of hugs and fuss.

What's happening in the picture?
Why do you think Gran came?

Who visits your house?
What happens when they arrive?
Why do they come?

Make a list of some of the people who come to your house. Remember to include people like the milkman and the postman. Draw a little picture beside each name.

Pin the list up on the wall and put a tick every time each person visits. Who comes most often?

Dad was off to work at the bank.
'Have a good day!' he called,
slamming the door behind him.

Mum was off to work driving her mini-bus.
'You just be good for your Gran, you two!
Do you hear me?'

Was it raining when Gran arrived?
Had it started to rain when Dad left?
What were Gran and Dad carrying?

Find a large piece of paper. Draw lines to divide it into four boxes. With help from Mum or Dad write one of these words in each box – rainy, cloudy, sunny, windy. Now draw a picture for each of the words.

Kerry and Mark helped Gran wash up.

'I wonder what's in that old shed,' Kerry said.

'Treasure, I expect!' said Mark.
'In a big wooden chest, with . . .'

'Let's have a look,' said Kerry.

How many birds can you see in the picture that are mostly yellow? Count them.
How many blue birds are sitting together on the branch?
How many blue birds are there altogether?
How many mostly green birds can you see?

How many birds can you see in Kerry and Mark's garden?

There was treasure in the shed.

It wasn't in a wooden chest though.

'Wow!' said Kerry. 'I bet people have been throwing their old junk in here for years! We can make anything with this!'

Can you see anything in the shed which is made of plastic? Or of wood? Or of metal?

One way of finding out what things are made of is to use a magnet. Find five or six objects outside your home. Which of them are attracted to the magnet? Draw pictures of them.

The things which are attracted to the magnet are made of metal that has iron or steel in it. Some metal objects are NOT attracted to a magnet. Can you find out what they are made of?

Kerry had a good idea.
She was a whizz with a few bits of junk.

She sorted out some wood and four old wheels.
Hammer, hammer, hammer she went. Fix, fix, fix.

'Cor!' said Mark. 'Let's go and show Rose!'

Do you know the song 'The Wheels on the Bus'? Can you make up a song about Kerry's cart? It could start 'The wheels on the cart go round and round' . . .

Go round your house. How many things can you find that have wheels? Look at your toys, then look outside too. Can you make a list of all the things? Write their names or draw a picture of each.

They sailed down Cherry Walk on Kerry's cart, to the house where Rose lived.

Ding, dong! Ding, dong! went the doorbell.

'Come and see Kerry's cart!' Mark called.

Try making a cart for one of your toys out of cardboard. Talk about it first – how can you fix the wheels on? What can you draw round to make the wheels?

When you've made it, tell someone how you did it. See if you can write some simple instructions, with pictures, so that someone else can make a cart like yours.

Rose and the twins danced up and down and round and about with excitement.
How they longed for a ride on the cart!

Charley's T-shirt is divided exactly into two different colours. What would you call each side of the T-shirt?

Wesley's T-shirt is divided into four colours. Each part is a quarter. Point to one quarter. Point to three quarters.

What else can you see in the picture that is divided into halves or quarters?

Beverley, their big sister, was looking after them. She shook her head. 'Sorry. Mum said you're not to go out in the street.'

How many people can you count in the picture?
If Kerry went off in the cart, how many people would be left in the picture?

If the twins went inside, how many people would there be in the picture?

If Kerry and Mark took Rose for a ride in the cart, how many children would be left in the picture?

'We'll all play here then,' said Charley.

'In our garden,' said Wesley.

'You can't do that,' Beverley said crossly. 'The band's coming. We don't want you disturbing us!'

'Not fair,' said Rose.

Find some of your toys that have wheels.

Set up a ramp. How far does each toy travel along a carpet when you let go of it at the top of the ramp?

Measure the distances in hand-spans.

Which goes the furthest?
Why do you think it was the best?
Is it still the best on a tiled or lino floor?

Ding, dong! Ding, dong!
went the doorbell.

'Here's the band!' shouted Wesley.

Kerry's eyes grew wider and wider
as she watched the girls come in
with their instruments.

Who has the biggest instrument?
Who has the smallest instrument?

Who has the fattest instrument?
Who has the thinnest instrument?

Count the number of instruments.
Does everyone have one instrument?
Is anyone holding more than one instrument?

Beverley's band went out to the garage. They set up their instruments and began to play.

Kerry tapped her feet to the music. Oh, how she would love to be the leader of a band!

Find an instrument in the picture
which is struck.
What is it hit with?
What type of sound does it make?

Look carefully at the other
instruments.
Can you find one that is plucked?
– one that is shaken?
– one that is blown?

Ding, dong! Ding, dong!
went the doorbell.

'Can't an old man have a bit of
peace and quiet in his own garden?'
grumbled Mr Johnson.

'That racket's frightening my birds.'

Are there times when a person might need to frighten away birds?

How does a farmer keep birds away from his fields?
Look for story books about scarecrows in the library.

See if you can make something that will scare the birds away. You could try a paper windmill, plastic cups tied to a string, coloured paper on a line, a scarecrow, balloons tied to a stick . . .

Beverley smiled nicely and said sorry and the girls' band closed the garage door tight to keep in the noise.

Kerry had another good idea. 'Why don't we go and play in our garden?' she said. 'Our Gran won't mind, honest.'

Why did Beverley close the doors tight?

Find some things which make a sound – what about a wind-up clock, a musical box, a digital alarm wrist-watch. Which is the noisiest? Which is the quietest? Can you put the things in order, starting with the loudest?

Put each thing into a saucepan. Is it quieter now? What happens when you put the lid on?

Beverley agreed, so the children zoomed up Cherry Walk on Kerry's cart.
'We're going to play in the garden, Gran,' Kerry said.

Gran smiled. 'Okay, love.'

Can you remember all the children's names?
What do you think it feels like to be riding along in Kerry's cart?

Why do you think Kerry wants to play in the shed?

How much can you remember of this story?
Who came to visit?
Where did Mum go?
Where did Dad go?
What did Kerry and Mark find in the shed?

Can you tell the story to someone else?

In no time at all Kerry had fixed up lots of noisy instruments.

'I'm the leader of the band!' she cried.

Gran came running down the garden.
'Hey! That's enough of that din!
You've woken the whole neighbourhood up!'

Perhaps Kerry's good idea wasn't quite so good after all!

Try making some musical instruments.

Striking sounds: find things which you can hit with a small stick. Try metal, plastic and wooden things – not glass. Try hitting them gently, then firmly; quickly, then slowly.

Plucking sounds: wrap some elastic bands around an empty box or pot and pluck them.

Shaking sounds: shake a box containing rice. Change the rice for something else, then change the box.

Activity notes

Pages 2–3 Making lists together is an enjoyable way for children to practise early writing skills. Keeping simple records, like the one suggested in the activity, will help in other subjects as well as English.

Pages 4–5 Young children don't always make the connection between the weather and its effects (eg on a windy day trees sway, leaves may be blown off). Drawing simple pictures will help them make those connections and is an early form of recording: an important scientific skill.

Pages 6–7 This activity is about simple addition. It also encourages children to follow different instructions and to look carefully at the picture.

Pages 8–9 In this activity your child is investigating the nature of materials. If you don't have an ordinary magnet, you could use magnetic letters or note holders. As a follow up, find out together which of these different materials can be recycled.

Pages 10–11 This activity incorporates both recording and observing skills. Encourage your child to think about why things have wheels and to look at the difference between wheels, eg on a toy car and a real car.

Pages 12–13 Making a cardboard cart will help your child to learn about planning and following instructions. Writing instructions for someone else to follow is writing for a real reason and purpose.

Pages 14–15 Simple work in fractions begins by dividing objects into two or four to create halves and quarters. Make sure your child understands that each part must be the same size to be a half or a quarter.

Pages 16–17 Children find it easier to understand subtraction by using real objects to begin with. Encourage them to talk about what they are doing, as they take away one item from a group.

Pages 18–19 Ask your child to guess which of the toys will go the furthest. They can test their ideas to see how accurate their guesses were. This activity also involves simple measuring. They could test further by putting small objects on the toys to make them heavier.

Pages 20–21 As children use comparative language to describe the height and width of objects, they will develop a feel for measure. Later on they will start using standard measures such as rulers and measuring tapes.

Pages 22–23 Sound can be made in a variety of ways, and instruments are generally grouped according to how to sound is created, eg wind instruments are blown, percussion instruments struck, string instruments plucked, and so on. Look through old magazines for pictures of instruments. Can your child match them with these words: strike, blow, pluck, shake?

Pages 24–25 Allowing children to plan their own investigations and to choose their own equipment is important. Give them plenty of time to make their bird-scarer and to try it out.

Pages 26–27 This activity involves comparing noise levels and testing different ways of muffling noise. Ask your child to suggest materials which they think will be good noise suppressors, eg paper, cotton wool, boxes. Try them out.

Pages 28–29 Recapping the story involves remembering and putting the events of the story into their correct sequence.

Pages 30–31 Pages 22–23 introduced the variety of ways in which sounds are made. Making instruments and describing their sounds will reinforce the idea. You can also investigate blowing sounds by making a bottle xylophone. Fill five or six bottles with different amounts of water and blow across the top of each one.

About the authors and advisers

Irene Yates is a writer and teacher in charge of language development at Lakey Lane School in Birmingham.

David Bell is Assistant Director of Education (Forward Planning) for Newcastle upon Tyne City Council, a former primary head and maths specialist.

Geoff Leyland is Deputy Head of Deer Park Primary School in Derbyshire and a former science and technology advisory teacher.

Mick Seller is Deputy Head of Asterdale Primary School in Derbyshire and a former science and technology advisory teacher.
Elizabeth Bassant is a language advisory teacher in Haringey, London. **Peter Ovens** is Principal Lecturer for Curriculum and Professional Development at Nottingham Polytechnic and a science specialist. **Peter Patilla** is a maths consultant, author and Senior Lecturer in Mathematics Education at Sheffield Polytechnic.
Margaret Williams is an advisory teacher for maths in Newton Abbott, Devon.

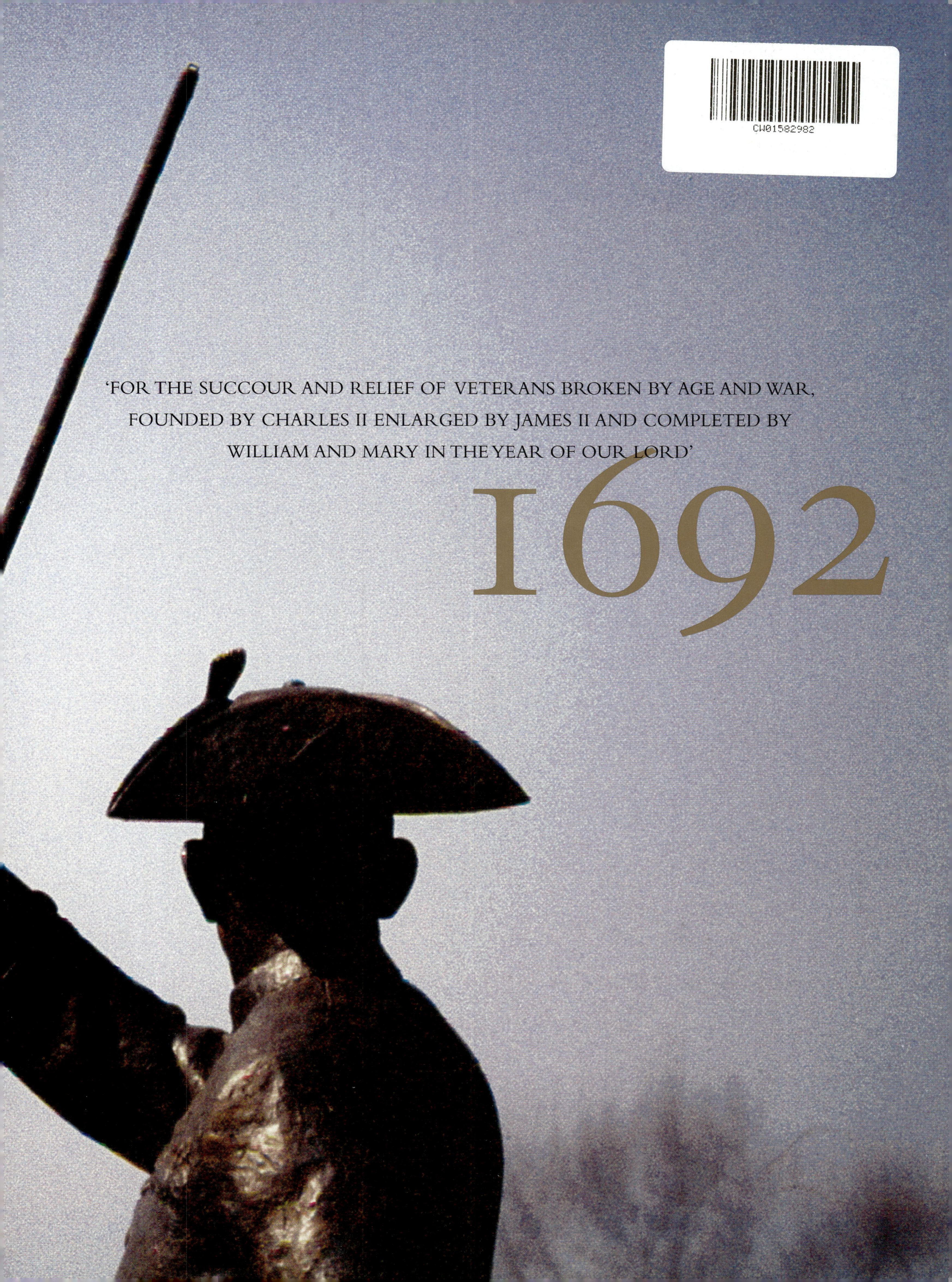

'FOR THE SUCCOUR AND RELIEF OF VETERANS BROKEN BY AGE AND WAR, FOUNDED BY CHARLES II ENLARGED BY JAMES II AND COMPLETED BY WILLIAM AND MARY IN THE YEAR OF OUR LORD'

1692

VISITING THE ROYAL HOSPITAL 5

LOOKING AFTER THE OLD SOLDIER 6

FOUNDATION OF THE ROYAL HOSPITAL 10

CONSTRUCTION AND OPENING 12

THE BUILDINGS 14

- BUILDINGS/SITE PLAN 15
- FIGURE COURT AND THE SOUTH TERRACE 16
- THE OCTAGON PORCH AND NORTH FRONT 20
- THE CHAPEL 22
- THE GREAT HALL 24
- THE LONG WARDS 26
- THE COUNCIL CHAMBER & STATE APARTMENTS 27
- THE WEST ROAD BUILDINGS 30
- COLLEGE COURT 31
- LIGHT HORSE COURT 32
- EAST ROAD BUILDINGS 33
- THE WELLINGTON HALL AND MUSEUM 34

THE GROUNDS 36

- THE RANELAGH GARDENS 38
- THE BURIAL GROUND AND BURTON'S COURT 39

LIFE AT THE ROYAL HOSPITAL 40

- A SOLDIER'S TALE 42
- IN-AND-OUT PENSIONERS 44
- ADMISSION TO THE ROYAL HOSPITAL 45
- FEMALE PENSIONERS 46
- RUNNING THE HOSPITAL 47
- HOSPITAL ADMINISTRATION 47
- DAILY LIFE 48
- THE INFIRMARY 53

CEREMONIES AND EVENTS 54

- FOUNDER'S DAY 54
- CAKE, CHEESE AND PUDDING 56
- THE CHELSEA FLOWER SHOW 57

ROYALTY 60

THE FUTURE 62

The author and publishers would like to thank Graham Smith at the National Army Museum, whose text is displayed at the Royal Hospital Museum Exhibition and the authors of previous guidebooks to the Hospital, whose work has been used for reference in this book.

QUE FRACTORUM CONDIDIT CAROLUS SECUNDUS
AUXIT JACOBUS SECUNDUS PERFECERE

VISITING THE ROYAL HOSPITAL

Welcome to the Royal Hospital - the home of the Chelsea Pensioners

The word 'hospital' means a place of 'refuge and shelter'. Established as a home over 300 years ago for soldiers who are unfit for duty as a result of injury or because of long service, it still serves its original purpose.

The Royal Hospital Chelsea is open to the public nearly every day of the year. Visitors may walk around most of the buildings and grounds and may gain access to the Great Hall, Chapel and Museum. (Opening times are published at the Chelsea and London gate entrances.)

Few other foundations can lay claim to have had so many eminent architects associated with them. Apart from Sir Christopher Wren (1632-1723) the Architect of the majority of the buildings seen today, several other famous architects have made contributions to the buildings on show today:

- Robert Adam (Clerk of Works from 1765-1792) changed all the windows to the sash windows seen today and remodelled many of the interiors of the staff apartments.
- Sir John Soane (Clerk of Works from 1807-1837) was responsible for most of the buildings now standing on the outer sides of the East and West Roads.
- Sir John Vanburgh designed the Orangery for Sir Robert Walpole.
- Thomas Leverton built Gordon House and
- Samuel Wyatt (Clerk of Works 1792-1806)

However, the most important contributors to the Royal Hospital are the Chelsea Pensioners. Some 25,000 old soldiers have lived at Chelsea and currently about 350 are provided with accommodation.
Please enjoy visiting their home.

LOOKING AFTER THE OLD SOLDIER

Until the 17th Century the state made no specific provision for old and injured soldiers. Care for the poor and sick was provided by the religious foundations. Most of this provision ended following the dissolution of the monasteries during the reign of King Henry VIII.

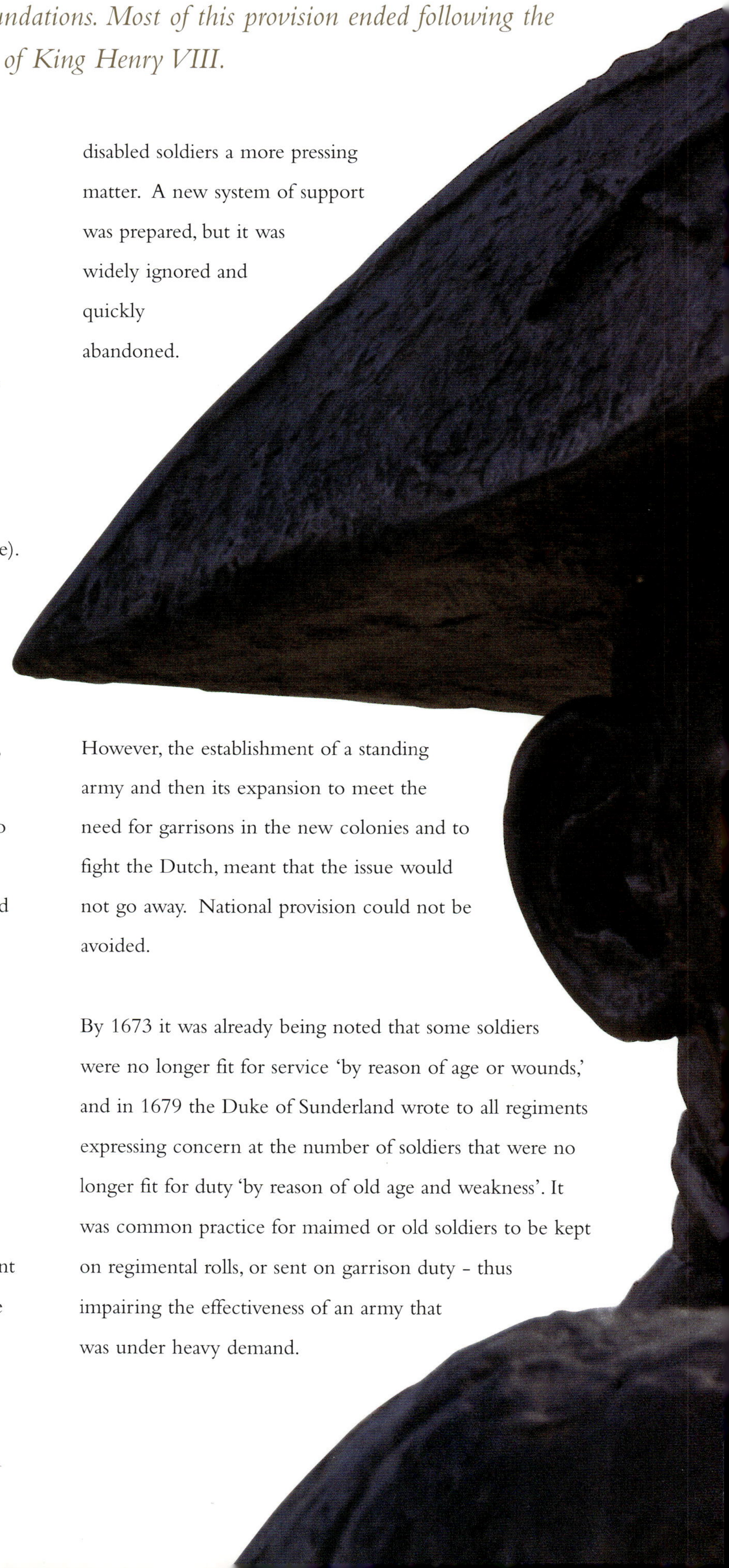

During the reign of Queen Elizabeth I, it became recognised that provision needed to be made for the poor and for sick and disabled soldiers. This led to an Act of Parliament, passed in 1593, that levied a weekly tax (not exceeding 6d in the pound) on parishes for the relief of soldiers and sailors who were 'maimed, hurt or grievously sick .. had lost their limbs or were disabled in their bodies' and so 'others may be encouraged to perform like endeavours'. In addition, there were proposals to establish almshouses for old soldiers (such as Lord Leicester's Almshouses in Warwick, which are still in their original use).

These arrangements do not appear to have been very satisfactory, as each parish sought to avoid its duties, but they continued in various guises until the mid-17th century. The Civil War, between Charles I and Parliament, which started in 1642, required changes to these arrangements - communities would not support those who had fought on the opposing side. Therefore, in 1645 Parliament decreed that pensions to disabled soldiers should be paid from national funds, not local taxation. Initially, money sequestered from the Royalists was used.

In 1651, the House of Commons ordered the Council of State to take care of maimed soldiers, but little action was taken except to provide accommodation in London in former barracks at Ely House and the Savoy.

The Restoration of Charles II in 1660, and the disbandment of the Parliamentary Army and exiled Royalist forces made the improvement of provision for the welfare of old or disabled soldiers a more pressing matter. A new system of support was prepared, but it was widely ignored and quickly abandoned.

However, the establishment of a standing army and then its expansion to meet the need for garrisons in the new colonies and to fight the Dutch, meant that the issue would not go away. National provision could not be avoided.

By 1673 it was already being noted that some soldiers were no longer fit for service 'by reason of age or wounds,' and in 1679 the Duke of Sunderland wrote to all regiments expressing concern at the number of soldiers that were no longer fit for duty 'by reason of old age and weakness'. It was common practice for maimed or old soldiers to be kept on regimental rolls, or sent on garrison duty - thus impairing the effectiveness of an army that was under heavy demand.

In 1680, Charles II granted a Royal Charter for the establishment of a Royal Hospital at Kilmainham, near Dublin for veterans of the Irish army (the English, Irish and Scots armies were then separate). The new hospital was funded by the stoppage of sixpence in the pound from the pay of the Irish troops.

The new standing army had been organised on the lines of the successful French army developed under Louis XIV. It was probably the establishment, in France, of the Hôtel des Invalides (founded in 1670) which influenced the decision to provide accommodation, rather than a system of pensions for old soldiers. The Hôtel des Invalides could accommodate some 5,000 disabled and superannuated officers and men and was visited twice by the Duke of Monmouth (the natural son of Charles II). The King also obtained plans of the building.

The only evidence to substantiate the legend that Charles II's mistress, Nell Gwyn, was at all involved in the founding of the Royal Hospital is the fact that it is denied in every history of the Royal Hospital. Her name is, however, recorded in the list of benefactors in the Great Hall.

King Charles was clearly determined to make provision for the soldiers on the English establishment and on 22nd December 1681, he issued a Royal Warrant authorising the building of the Royal Hospital 'to begin so excellent a work that he should proceed with his own hospital, for the succour and relief of Veterans broken by Age and War'.

'IF I FORGET THEE

DO NOT FORGET ME’

King Charles II

On 16th February 1682 'the King in his owne person laid the first stone for a hospital for maimed soldiers at Chelsey'. This stone has not been found

Sir Christopher Wren

Sir Stephen Fox

FOUNDATION OF *The Royal Hospital*

Sir Christopher Wren, Charles II's Surveyor-General of Works, was commissioned to design and erect the buildings. Sir Stephen Fox (1627-1716), who had been Paymaster General to the Army from 1661-1679, and was a Commissioner of the Treasury, was commissioned to secure the funds necessary to progress the scheme.

Charles II was always short of money and Parliament had made it quite clear that it would not fund the project. Fox therefore sought funding from private donations. The King provided £6,787 4s 2½d from unused money for the 'secret service'. Other contributions came to about £13,000 (including Fox's land purchase). This was clearly insufficient to fund the new project and Fox therefore proposed a novel method of securing funds. As Paymaster General Fox had been responsible for paying the army. To do this on time, he borrowed the money. From 1668 to 1679 he had received 12/- in the £ for performing this service. When he resigned this position, because of 'difficulties' the money was reallocated by King Charles - 4d to pay for the costs of paying the army and 8d to reduce the costs of the pay. Fox suggested that the money saved should go to the Royal Hospital. In 1683 the King agreed to allocate 4d to the Royal Hospital, backdated to 1680/81. This was later increased to the whole of the 12d, less the actual costs of paying the army.

The funds thus provided were still insufficient and Fox had to find other sources of funding. A levy of 12d in the £ was made on the sale of officers' commissions and from 1684 a day's pay was deducted from every officer and soldier in the army. The last measure was, in effect, a contributory pension, as all soldiers were to benefit.

In 1685, Wren, who was also an MP, proposed that the fees from the licensing of Hackney carriages should accrue to the Royal Hospital. This was approved although no income has ever been received. In the same year, the City of Newcastle-upon-Tyne also agreed to supply 100 chaldrons (wagons) of coal each year to the Royal Hospital in lieu of paying rent to the Crown for the castle there. This continued until 1807.

Fox also guaranteed the loans and contracts 'which made him be out of purse about Six thousand pounds for which he never took interest, because it was a charity'.

The chosen site, set adjacent to the River Thames in the pastoral setting of Chelsea, contained the uncompleted building of the former 'Chelsey Colledge', a theological college founded by James I in 1610. Never having been successful the College was closed during the Civil War and was later used to house prisoners during the Civil War and in the later wars against the Dutch. In 1667, the site was given by Charles II to the Royal Society (another of his imaginative creations). The Society, of which both Fox and Wren were members (Wren was President in 1681), had found no use for it and on February 8th 1682, it was repurchased by the King (or rather by Sir Stephen Fox on his behalf) for the reasonable sum of £1,300.

View from the River Thames (model)

S
N

CONSTRUCTION AND OPENING

Wren's design for the Royal Hospital is based on the Hôtel des Invalides. The original building was intended to house 412 veteran soldiers and their officers and comprised a single quadrangle, known as Figure Court, surrounded on two sides by the accommodation blocks and on a third by the hall and chapel. The pavilions at each corner provided for the kitchen, infirmary and officers' accommodation.

The early building continued at a rapid pace, so much so that Charles II was able to inspect the work, including the partly completed chapel, just before his death in 1685 and proudly proclaim 'that Fox and Hee (Wren) had done that great worke without the help of the Treasury, who indeed never gave the least countenance toward it'.

Even before work had begun it was realised that the buildings would be insufficient and Wren added two further quadrangles to his design (similar to Les Invalides). In 1686, the construction of the new quadrangles on each flank was approved (now known as Light Horse and College Courts).

The whole project could have been jeopardised by James II's ill-conceived appointment of Richard Jones, the Earl of Ranelagh (1638-1712), as Paymaster-General of the Forces, an office he held from 1685-1702. Owing to his mismanagement and embezzlement there was continued delay in completing the building work and admitting the pensioners. Among his misdemeanours, he diverted funds intended for completing the Royal Hospital to the building of a 'small but lavish' house (sadly demolished in the 19th century) in the grounds and he was allowed to appropriate about a third of the Royal Hospital's land for his own uses at an annual payment of £5. Following his dismissal from office in 1702, it was discovered that he had been guilty of gross fraud and had misappropriated a total of £904,000 from army funds. Such was his degree of mismanagement that the Royal Hospital's accounts for the period from 1692 to 1702 were not closed until 1737.

Ranelagh, died 'very poor and needy' in 1712 but left a legacy to the Royal Hospital to provide scarlet coats for the In-Pensioners and a cash gift on Founder's Day. Unfortunately, the Royal Hospital invested this unwisely and lost it in the financial collapse of the 'South Sea Bubble' in 1720.

In 1692, work was finally completed and Ranelagh was compelled to allow pensioners in. On February 4th, the first group of 99 In-Pensioners were installed and on March 28th, the full complement of 476 was made up when they were joined by a further 377 residents.

THE BUILDINGS

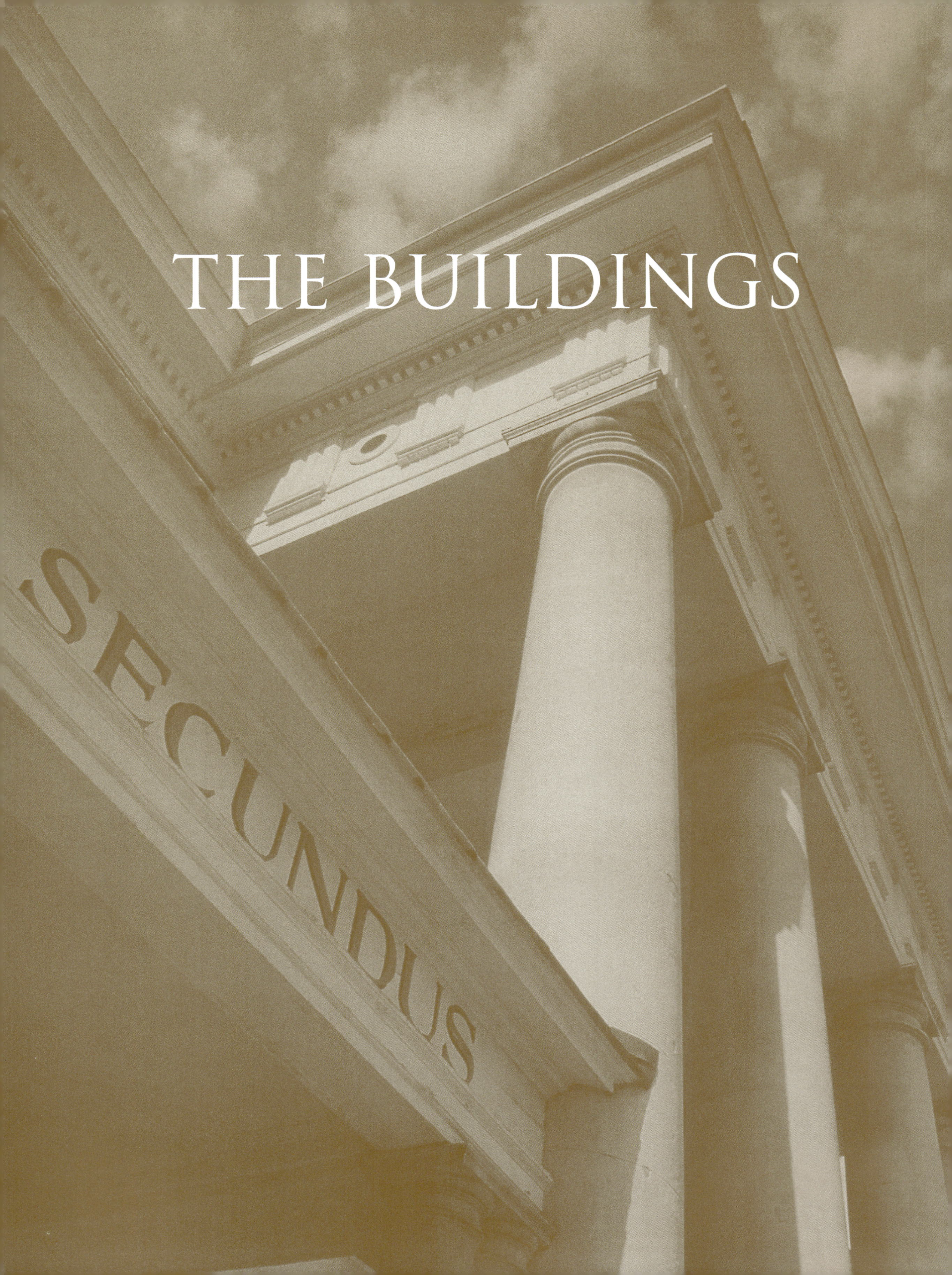

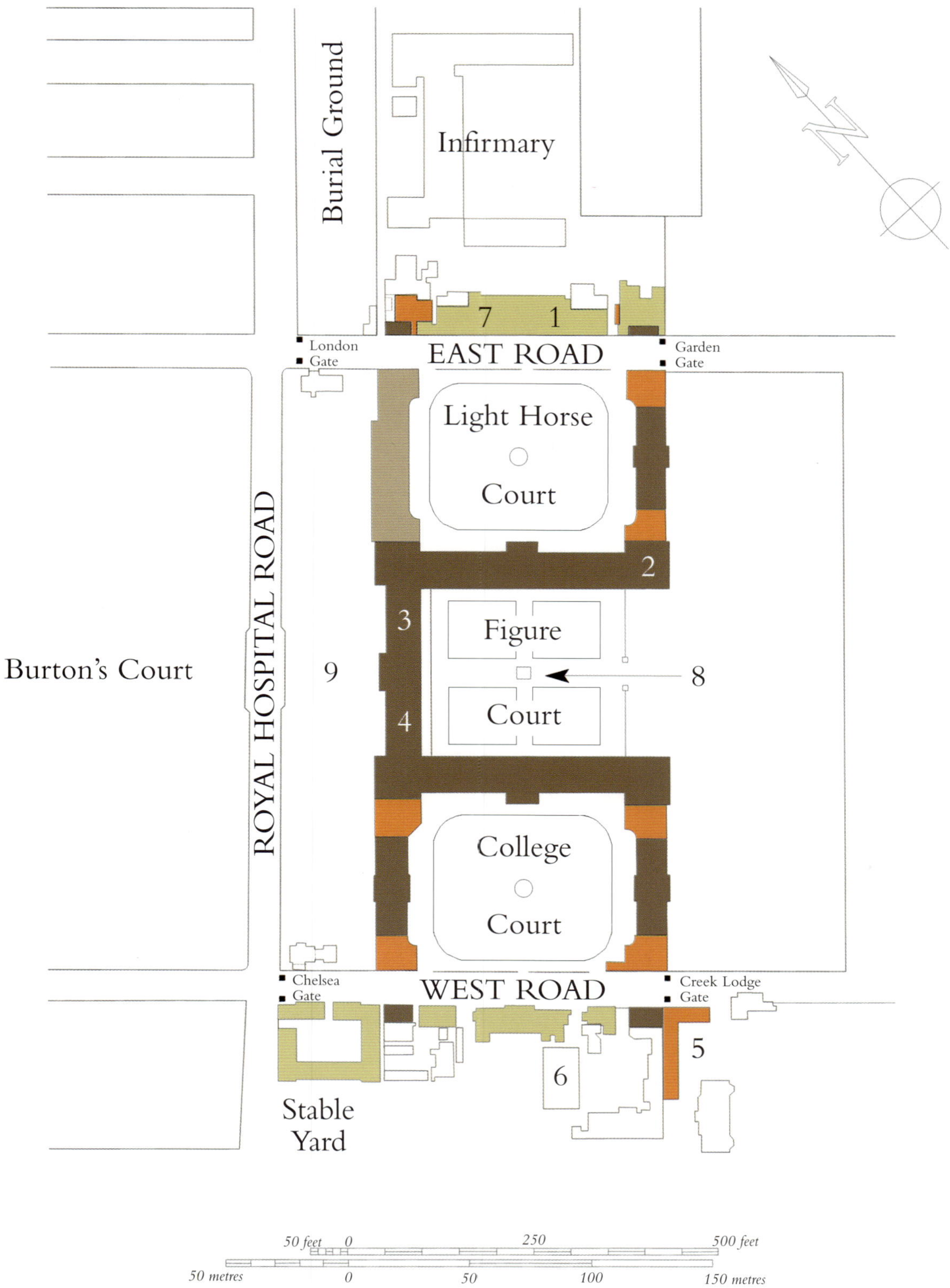

Wren buildings

Wren reproduction buildings

Eighteenth-century buildings

Soane buildings

1. Governor's and Lieutenant-Governor's offices
2. State Apartments
3. Chapel
4. Great Hall
5. Library and Roman Catholic Chapel
6. Prince of Wales Hall
7. Museum and Shop
8. Statue of Charles II by Grinling Gibbons
9. Statue of a Pensioner by Philip Jackson

FIGURE COURT

The gilded statue of King Charles II, from which Figure Court takes its name

FIGURE COURT AND THE SOUTH TERRACE

The 7'6" statue of Charles II, from which the Court takes its name, is the work of Grinling Gibbons. It shows the king as a Roman general, holding a baton as a sign of his Imperial authority. He does not have the customary wig and moustache, and with its bare arms and legs, it must have been considered daring. It was presented to the King by Tobias Rustat, a long-time retainer, in 1682 and was moved to the Royal Hospital after the King died in 1685. It was placed in its current position at about the time the first pensioners were admitted. Originally gilded it was bronzed in 1782, but has been re-gilded to commemorate Queen Elizabeth II's Golden Jubilee in 2002.

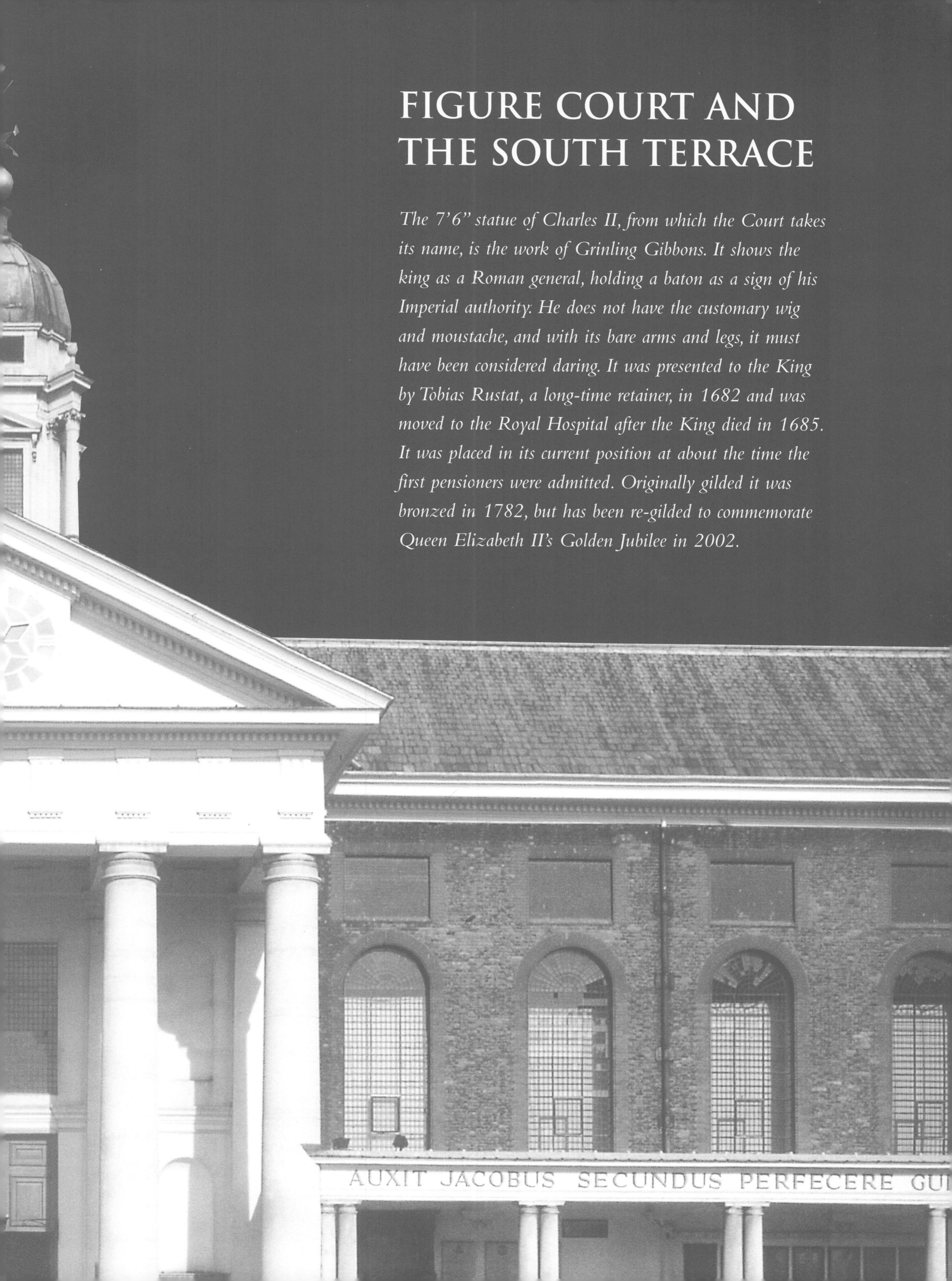

FIGURE COURT AND THE SOUTH TERRACE

This is the oldest part of the Royal Hospital and was begun by Wren in 1682. It is enclosed by buildings on its northern, eastern and western sides, but its southern end lies open to the grounds and the river. The northern range contains the Chapel and the Great Hall, with an Octagon vestibule between them. The colonnade which extends over the whole length of the range on its inner side is surmounted by a cornice bearing a Latin inscription (see the preface), said to have been composed by Wren himself.

The colonnade is all Wren's original work, the benches and panelling dating from 1688. The double columns, joined at the base, were not used by Wren elsewhere. The Doric columns of the main portico, 32' high, support the Royal Hospital's water cistern. This was originally filled from the River Thames.

The South Terrace overlooks the South Grounds. These were originally laid out as water gardens and meadows. Flooding, and the need to construct the Chelsea Embankment, led to their levelling in 1850. The retaining wall was demolished and much of the original terrace removed, but the terminal walls and gateways with their wrought-iron gates by Jean Tijou, have been preserved. In the grounds are two batteries of guns. That on the left is composed of four French guns captured at Waterloo (1815). The other is formed of two guns taken from the Sikhs at Chillianwallah (1849), one Chinese piece (from about 1680), and one Dutch gun dated 1623. The 36" spherical shells were designed for use with Mallet mortars (mid-19th century), but were never actually employed in action.

Main picture opposite: The South Terrace

This page (top): Colonnade's Latin Inscription

Left: One of the guns

Bottom row of pictures: Statue of Charles II; Benches; Double columns; Batteries of guns; a Chelsea pensioner; Benches

The guns on display at The Royal Hospital are on loan from The Royal Armouries.

THE

SOUTH TERRACE

DIEV·ET·MON·DROIT

THE OCTAGON PORCH AND NORTH FRONT

The octagon supports the Royal Hospital's distinctive cupola and lantern. This rises to a height of 130'. Over the north entrance is the Royal coat of arms, removed from the Royal Hospital at Kilmainham at its closure in 1925.

Here, and in the Great Hall, are displayed the staves of flags and standards mainly captured in wars in India, Africa and China. The 95 original colours, which were deposited at the Royal Hospital by order of William IV in 1835, have mainly decayed. Those now hanging in the Great Hall, from the Napoleonic wars, are reproductions.

The entrance to the porch from the north, or Royal Hospital Road side, is flanked by four British field guns, three Victorian and one Georgian.

The Statue of a Chelsea Pensioner, by Philip Jackson, was unveiled in 2000 to commemorate the Millennium. The In-Pensioner, shown at one and a half times life size, is worn by war and bent by age, but still stands proud. About the base is the soldiers' prayer, based on that said by Sir Jacob Astley before the Battle of Edgehill (1642) - 'O Lord you know how occupied I shall be this day. If I forget thee do not forget me'.

Main picture opposite: The Octagon Porch
This page (top and bottom):
Statue of a Chelsea Pensioner

THE CHAPEL

Work on the Chapel started in 1681 and was completed in 1687. It is a rare example of Wren's pure ecclesiastical work, being carried out without site constraints. It was designed to accommodate about 500 people, all the staff and pensioners, and rises 42' high.

The wainscoting and pews (originally for staff and Horse Guards) are by Sir Charles Hopson, the leading joiner of his day and deputy Clerk of Works at the Royal Hospital from 1691-1698. The choir stalls are modern additions. Backs have been fitted to the benches, and the three-decker pulpit has been dismantled to make the existing pulpit and reading-desk, otherwise the original plan is maintained. The plasterwork was carried out by Henry Margetts. The carving is by William Emmett, Master Carver before Grinling Gibbons and William Morgan. The organ case is the work of Renatus Harris, but his organ has been replaced by a modern instrument.

The painting of the Resurrection in the half dome of the apse is by Sebastiano Ricci, assisted by his nephew Marco, and dates from 1714. The work was probably paid for, as a donation to the Royal Hospital, by Queen Anne.

The Royal Hospital's magnificent silver-guilt altar plate (not on display) was made by Ralph Leete and is hallmarked 1687-1688. It comprises a large alms dish, a pair of candlesticks with baluster stems, a salver, three flagons, four chalices and patens, and a straining spoon. The altar cross, the font and the coat of arms on the front of the organ loft date from 1955-1956.

One of the original service books has been preserved. The old registers of baptisms, marriages and burials are now held at the Public Records Office. Burial services were discontinued in 1854, and weddings which were uncommon after 1753 were banned from 1815-1919. The first televised church service in Britain was broadcast from the Chapel in 1949.

The Chapel was consecrated in August 1691, and compulsory services held twice daily. Nowadays, they are normally confined to the Sunday morning service before which the In-Pensioners parade in Figure Court. Visitors are welcome at Sunday Services.

Opposite and right: Inside The Chapel
This page (top): the Font; the Coat of Arms; the pulpit; close-up of the Resurrection by Ricci

IHS

THE GREAT HALL

Until the early 19th Century, the Great Hall was the dining room and was furnished with sixteen long tables (one for each Ward). In 1782 these were sawn in half and arranged in two rows along each side of the hall, with the Governor's table on the dais at the far end. Each table would provide space for two sergeants, two corporals, a drummer and twenty-one private soldiers (in all twenty six, the number that lodged in each Long Ward).

Various pictures: Inside The Great Hall
Bottom right (inset): 5 gallon 'black jack'

THE GREAT HALL

Although the kitchen was placed by Wren adjacent to the Great Hall, there was no connection until 1824. Prior to that, all the food was conveyed along the Colonnade and through the main entrance. Heating was provided by an open fire in the middle of the room.

Towards the end of the eighteenth century the Pensioners took to dining in the Wards and from the early 19th century, all food was collected from the kitchen. The Great Hall was then used for recreation, courts martial and Army entrance examinations. It was here that the Duke of Wellington's body lay in state in 1852 - as Sir Arthur Wellesley, he had been arraigned in the same place before the Court of Inquiry into the Convention of Cintra in 1809. The table on which his coffin rested is just inside the entrance. On it rest two 5 gallon 'black jacks', leather jugs formerly used for bringing ale up from the beer cellar below.

In 1955 the Hall was restored to its original purpose, and oak benches have since been replaced by chairs.

The large mural painting at the far end dates from about 1690 and represents Charles II on horseback surrounded by allegorical figures, with the Royal Hospital buildings in the background. It was begun by Antonio Verrio, but is mainly the work of Henry Cooke. It was restored in 2002. The portraits of George II and Queen Caroline are by Enoch Seeman (1739). Those of George III (1767) and Queen Charlotte (1762) are by Allan Ramsay. The equestrian portrait of John, Duke of Marlborough (c.1702) by John Closterman, which hangs in the gallery over the door, was presented by the Drapers' Company in 1954. The other 17th and 18th century paintings are mainly copies of originals by Kneller. William III's coat of arms, displayed on the front of the gallery, was carved by William Emmett.

THE LONG WARDS

The four-storeyed Wings enclosing the East and West sides of Figure Court contain the In-Pensioners' living quarters, which are known as Long Wards. The original berths, as designed by Wren, measured 6' (1.8 metres) square. Each berth was provided with a bed, a straw mattress, a flock mattress, two pairs of sheets, three blankets and a coverlet. There was barely any space for furnishings which included a wooden chest, mounted on castors with a padlock and key and a built-in table fitted with a drawer.

Originally washing facilities were provided in each Long Ward. All the toilets ('privvies') were located at the end of each outer courtyard where they could be easily emptied. For night use, each Ward therefore had eight brass pails, along with a pewter bedpan for the Sergeant. Lighting was provided by nine 'lanthornes' in each Ward, but due to the risk of fire the use of candlesticks was stopped in 1769. Gas lighting was installed in 1854, but it was not until the early 20th century when electricity was substituted for gas, was there any lighting in the berths.

The East and West Wings are symmetrically planned, with a pair of Long Wards arranged back-to-back on each of the four floors. Each Long Ward is 200' (61 metres) long with a line of wainscoted berths running down the inner side, now containing eighteen berths.

The stairs at the northern ends were designed to be shallow and wide for the convenience of the older and infirm. The staircase in the East Wing is modern, having been damaged by bombing in 1940. The wood used to repair it was left over from the repair of the House of Commons and the repaired wall is picked out in lighter brick. Wren provided separate stairs at the south end of each Wing as a means of escape in case of fire.

Each Long Ward contains two fireplaces, which during the 19th century were fitted with ranges and were, until 1955, used for the cooking of rations. In 1778 the Clerk of Works, Robert Adam converted the oak benches which stood before the fireplaces into settles, but none survive. Central heating was installed from 1928 and lifts from 1926.

The berths were enlarged in 1954 -1955 and again in 1991 to their present size of 9' by 9' (2.7 by 2.7 metres). In addition, the berths were roofed over and better lighting and ventilation installed. Each berth is now furnished with a bed, a table, a chair, a wardrobe and a chest of drawers, together with a bedside light, radio and television point. Complete privacy can be secured by closing the berth door and shutter. A mock up of a berth is on show in the Museum.

The facilities are being upgraded to meet the needs of the 21st century In-Pensioner. Improvements to bathing and WC facilities are planned and an IT suite has been opened. However, all the works have to take account of the historic structure. Improved access arrangements for In-Pensioners with disabilities is also planned.

Top: The Long Wards
Bottom: A typical berth

THE COUNCIL CHAMBER AND STATE APARTMENTS

These rooms are open to visitors by special arrangement. The most important is the Council Chamber, which, unusually, is one and a half stories high (this may be seen from Figure Court) and seems to have been intended as the dining room for visiting Royalty. It was given over to the Board of Commissioners in 1686, but the Board continued to meet in the Royal Hospital's office at Scotland Yard until 1797. Thereafter, the Board met in a room in College Court (now the Snooker Room) and did not start to use the Council Chamber until 1946. In the intervening period the room was maintained as part of the Governor's apartments, which occupy the floors above.

The heavily moulded ceiling, displaying James II's cipher, is by John Grover, *the wainscoting* by William Cleere and *the fine lime wood carving* over the fireplace by William Emmett. The room was redecorated by Robert Adam in 1776 and *the chimney-piece, gilt girandoles (mirrors to enhance candle light),* some tables and *the state chair* date from this period. The portrait group of Charles I and his family is by the school of Van Dyck. There are portraits by Lely of Charles II and Queen Catherine, James Duke of York, and the Earl of Ranelagh; by Kneller of William III, (possibly) by Mary Beale of Sir Stephen Fox, and by Jacomb-Hood (after Kneller) of Sir Christopher Wren. The Council Chamber may be hired for private functions.

Other rooms in this area are the Ante Rooms, also on the Ground Floor, which contains paintings of Queen Anne by George Murray and an early view of the Royal Hospital by Maas (c. 1719). The Governor's Apartments, above the Council Chamber, contain the 'Adam Suite' - rooms remodelled by Robert Adam and the Surveyor's Closet (three rooms), which provided Wren's accommodation and office when the Royal Hospital was under construction.

A variety of splendid artefacts inside The Council Chamber

THE WEST ROAD BUILDINGS

Most of Wren's buildings in the West Road have been pulled down. The old 'Rear Guardhouse' is now used as offices for the Surveyor of Works (note the old style of leaded lights) still survives, along with the old Barber's Shop (now a private dwelling) and two cottages at the southern end of the road.

When Robert Walpole became Paymaster General in 1714, he appropriated (in the style of the Earl of Ranelagh) four and a half acres of Royal Hospital land (from the entrance gate to the River Thames) and enlarged the rear part of Wren's stable block to provide himself with a house. Walpole, who is generally acknowledged as the first Prime Minister from 1721-1742, maintained the property until his death in 1745.

The current buildings were erected mainly by Sir John Soane from 1809-1822. They mainly comprise the present Chelsea Gate Guard-house (originally a smoking room), the new Stable-Yard buildings (1814-1817) (which occupy half the space covered by Wren's buildings) and the large building opposite College Court. This was planned to house the Washhouse and the Surgeon's House and is now occupied by the Quartermaster's Department and the Organist.

The Gateway with stone piers

The Prince of Wales Hall, an amenity centre (including the Barber's shop), was added behind the Quartermaster's building in 1985. It stands near to the site of the Whitster's House - a Wren building constructed for the laundry. The post of Whitster only became defunct in recent years. The Bakehouse (there were four at various times) and original Barber's shop were also in this area.

In 1809, Soane constructed a new Infirmary building, with space for 80 patients (the Infirmary was damaged by bombing in the Second World War and later demolished). The site is now occupied by the National Army Museum (1968 - 1969).

At the southern end of the West Road, a gateway with stone piers and handsome wrought-iron gates gives access to the old Greenhouse, or Orangery, built by Sir John Vanburgh for Walpole in about 1725. The building which is L-shaped, had been used for a variety of purposes over the years and fell into decay. In 1962-1963 the exterior was faithfully restored and the interior converted to new uses. The long arm of the 'L' now houses the Library, and the short arm has been converted into the Roman Catholic Chapel.

Part of Walpole's land was repossessed by the Royal Hospital for Soane's Infirmary, but the rest was let on lease in 1809 to a Colonel Gordon whose house, since enlarged and used as staff quarters, was built by Thomas Leverton, an architect of the Adam School.

The Prince of Wales Hall looking towards College Court

COLLEGE COURT

College Court (originally Infirmary Court) was one of the two new quadrangles added by Wren in 1686. The well head at the centre dates from 1722.

The buildings are smaller in scale than the original ranges, following the design of the Hôtel des Invalides. The northern range supplied accommodation for staff and additional dining halls for the Light Horse and Guards.

The southern range is built on the foundations of the Chelsea College building. This range was to provide the Infirmary and Surgery. During the Napoleonic wars, the Infirmary was taken over for injured serving soldiers and sick In-Pensioners were banished to a temporary facility above the Great Hall until Soane built the new Infirmary. This block has since been converted for staff accommodation.

There was also a school for the daughters of In-Pensioners from 1729-1862. The girls provided the Chapel choir.

Light Horse Court

Like College Court, this quadrangle was added by Wren for James II in 1687-1688. It was originally a plain gravelled yard, and the fine wrought-iron cage and lamp-post (1722) in the centre protected a well, which was provided for watering horses. The roadway with its stone posts and chains was laid out by Soane in 1819.

LIGHT HORSE COURT & EAST ROAD BUILDINGS

LIGHT HORSE COURT

The Court takes its name from the Light Horse (cavalry) whose needs were not considered in the original proposal. They were junior to the old soldiers of the Horse Guards (who occupied a pavilion in the East Wing), but senior to the infantry. Such differences were abolished in 1850.

The North-East wing provided a number of officers' quarters. This range was heavily damaged with some loss of life, by enemy bombing in 1918. It was reconstructed in 1923 only to be destroyed again by a V2 rocket in 1945. This instance of history repeating itself is commemorated by a plaque on the west side of the East Road. After the Second World War reconstruction was long delayed, but in 1964-1965, the unsightly ruins gave place to an exact reproduction of the original exterior. The interior arrangements are, however, quite different, and the new building is currently occupied by additional Long Wards providing 64 additional places. It is intended to provide a temporary Infirmary in this building from 2004-2006 during the construction of a new Infirmary.

The single storey screen walls linking the various ranges are part of Wren's original design. Provided to give accommodation for storerooms and the Royal Hospital's privvies (the last of which was removed in 1854). Doors and windows have since been added to allow other uses.

EAST ROAD BUILDINGS

Although at first glance this seems to be a single range of buildings, parts date from the 17th and 19th centuries. The small building next to the Burial Ground, originally the Main Guardhouse, and the corresponding building at the far end of the road, are both by Wren (and are now private residences). The range of buildings connecting them, which contains the Secretary's Office and the Museum, stand on what was formerly part of the Governor's garden. It was added by Soane in 1817-1819 to accommodate the 51 clerks required on account of the increased number of army pensioners after the Napoleonic wars. The administration of all army pensions continued to be carried out in this office and numerous temporary outbuildings, until responsibility for out-pensions was transferred to the new Army Pensions Office set up by the War Office in 1955. The original built-in filing cupboards and safes have been preserved. The building provides accommodation for the Royal Hospital's administrative offices together with the Museum.

The Wellington Hall and Museum

A small Royal Hospital Museum, composed of artefacts left by deceased In-Pensioners, opened in the Great Hall in 1866. The current Museum opened in 1960. The Entrance Hall is dedicated to the memory of the Duke of Wellington, and a variety of objects associated with him are to be seen in it, including six French 'Eagles', George Jones' panorama of the Battle of Waterloo (1820) and a portrait of the Duke by John Simpson. There is also a contemporary painting of Queen Elizabeth II by Andrew Festing (1998).

In the Wellington Hall, a diorama depicts The Royal Hospital in about 1742. This shows the Royal Hospital as it was when Ranelagh's land had been turned to commercial use and Walpole had acquired the site on the west side. The original water gardens may also be seen.

Leading from the Hall, the gallery contains the main Museum displays and exhibitions. Because it is not possible to visit the Long Wards, a reconstruction of a typical berth has been provided. *The uniform of a veteran soldier* is also displayed. Invalid units of Pensioners were created from 1703, formed from those who were claiming a pension but found fit for duty. Usually disbanded during peacetime, there were 66 companies found by the Royal Hospital when the invalids were converted in 'Garrison' battalions in 1803.

The collection of medals has been built up from those of deceased In-Pensioners who bequeathed them to the Hospital or had no relatives to claim them, and totals over 2,100.

The Museum has recently had two major additions. *The parade chair* was presented to Queen Elizabeth II by the Royal Hospital to commemorate her Golden Jubilee in 2002. The chair, which the Queen uses for public events, is retained in the Museum for public display.

The Sovereign's Mace was presented to the Royal Hospital by Queen Elizabeth II, on 5th July 2002. Throughout its existence the Royal Hospital has had no colours or other distinctive device. The Mace is now carried at all the Royal Hospital's ceremonial events.

A French 'Eagle' captured at Martinique in 1809

RH

SEBASTOPOL

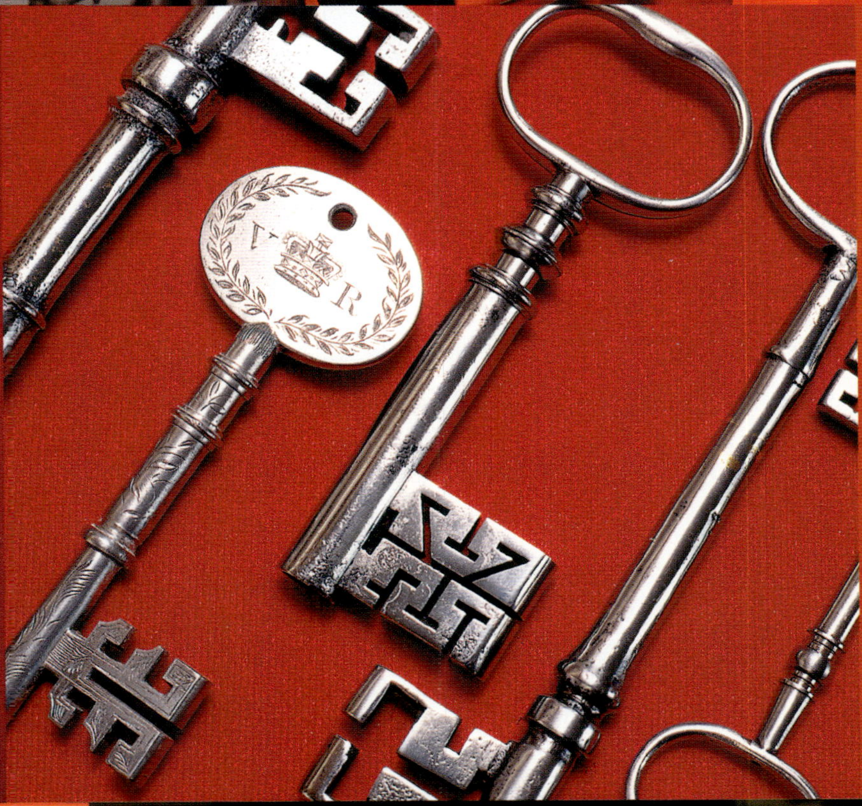

THE GROUNDS

The Chelsea College site for the new Royal Hospital had been purchased by Sir Stephen Fox out of his own pocket. Additional land was purchased in James II's reign making a site of about 66 acres.

THE RANELAGH GARDENS

In 1688, The Earl of Ranelagh persuaded Wren to build him a house to the east of the South Terrace. He then leased 23 acres of Royal Hospital land for a period of 99 years at a rental of £5, as recompense for lands lost in his native Ireland. The land thus acquired included the whole of the east side of the current Royal Hospital plus the site now occupied by Chelsea Barracks. After his fall from power and death in poverty in 1712, his daughter Lady Catherine Jones, continued to live in Ranelagh House with the help of influential friends. All the land was sold off, in ten lots, in 1733.

In 1739, a speculative builder bought Ranelagh House and its grounds and in 1741, in partnership with the owner of the Drury Lane Theatre, built the Rotunda and associated pleasure grounds (against much objection from the Royal Hospital). Opening in 1742 the wooden Rotunda was designed by William Jones. With an external diameter of 185' (56 metres - slightly smaller than the Albert Hall), it was regarded as an engineering masterpiece. The Rotunda was the venue of much public entertainment, including breakfasts, concerts, masquerades and fireworks. The gardens were described as having winding paths, ornamental canals, water features and groves. It eventually went out of favour and both the Rotunda and Ranelagh House were demolished in 1805.

A small part of Ranelagh's land was repurchased by the Board of Commissioners using the remains of the legacy that he left.

Wren's magnificent formal gardens, provided a vista from the Royal Hospital to the River Thames, which included canals gazebos and summer houses (one each for the Governor and Lieutenant Governor). However, these were all swept away from 1850-1868 when the Chelsea Embankment was constructed.

The present Ranelagh Gardens (on the site of Ranelagh House and the Rotunda), were laid out by John Gibson (who designed Battersea Park and several other Royal parks) in about 1860. Previously, the area had been used for Pensioners' gardens and Soane provided a shelter for their use in 1834. This structure was restored in 2003.

Much of the rest was bought back during the 19th century, as was the land taken by Walpole. The Royal Hospital also benefited in acquiring land as a result of the construction of the Chelsea Embankment and Chelsea Bridge Road. The Royal Hospital site now covers a total of 66 acres (27 hectares).

The South Grounds are the venue annually of the Chelsea Flower Show.

The Soane Pavilion, recently restored

THE BURIAL GROUND AND BURTON'S COURT

The Burial Ground lies between the London Gate entrance and Chelsea Bridge Road. The plot was consecrated in August 1691, and closed in December 1854. Between those dates over 10,000 pensioners and staff of the Royal Hospital were buried there, including William Cheselden, the pioneer of modern surgery and Dr Burney, Organist at the Royal Hospital from 1783-1814 and author of the once famous General History of Music, though perhaps he is now better known as the father of Fanny Burney, the novelist and friend of Dr. Johnson. Burials took place at Brompton Cemetery from 1855 until 1893, since then the Royal Hospital has had its own burial and interment grounds at Brookwood Cemetery, near Woking.

On the north side of Royal Hospital Road, which was driven across the Hospital property in 1846, lies Burton's Court, bounded on the far side by St Leonard's Terrace. Burton's Court was originally a hayfield. Flanked by the Porter's Lodge and the old Fore Guardhouse, are the main entrance gates to the Royal Hospital. These are approached along Royal Avenue, which was originally laid out to communicate with the King's (private) Road and was intended only for use on state occasions. If continued in a straight line, Royal Avenue would have reached Kensington Palace, the home of King William III and Queen Mary. Whether such a link, with the benefits of providing ready access from the Palace to the River Thames, was envisaged by Wren as part of a more grand design, can only be conjectured.

LIFE AT
THE ROYAL HOSPITAL

A SOLDIER'S TALE

In the museum hangs the portrait of William Hiseland by George Alsop. Hiseland is the oldest recorded In-Pensioner and died in 1732 aged 112 years old. His remarkable military career spanned from the Battle of Edgehill in 1642, through the Irish Wars under William III to the Flanders campaigns under the Duke of Marlborough at the beginning of the 18th century. He became an In-Pensioner in 1713.

Hiseland is just one of the many thousand of In-Pensioners who played their part in the military campaigns of the last three centuries. Today a number of volunteer In-Pensioners act as Royal Hospital guides. Apart from informing visitors about the history of the Royal Hospital, they are able to relate some of their own real life experiences.

The reminiscences of a number of In-Pensioners are currently published in books such as ***'Before They Fade'*** *and* ***'Soldiers'.***

William Hiseland, the oldest recorded In-Pensioner

IN AND OUT PENSIONERS

The term 'Chelsea Pensioner' has been used over the centuries to describe both 'In-' and 'Out-Pensioners'. An In-Pensioner is simply one who resides in the Royal Hospital Chelsea. On entry, he surrenders the whole of his army pension. An Out-Pensioner is a former soldier of the Regular Army and receives a pension for long service and/or disability caused through service.

The term derives from the period when the Royal Hospital was still being built. James II, who succeeded King Charles in 1685, made the first attempt to put Army pensions on a systematic basis in 1689. He decreed that a daily allowance should be made to all soldiers disabled by wounds or accidents, who had become unfit for service or who had served for 20 years. The payment of pension claims had to be approved by the Board of Commissioners at the Royal Hospital. In March 1689-1690, before the Royal Hospital was open, there were 579 pensioners approved and they were termed 'Out-Pensioners'.

When the first 476 'In-Pensioners' were admitted in 1692 the number of Out-Pensioners was small. In 1703 there were as few as 51. However, the increasing size of the standing army meant that the number of Out-Pensioners rose steadily - from 739 in 1708, to 14,700 in 1763 (after the Seven Years War) and 36,757 in 1815.

The Royal Hospital remained responsible for all army pensions until 1955.

ADMISSION TO THE ROYAL HOSPITAL

In 1685, James II laid down the conditions for admission to the Royal Hospital:-

'All non-commission officers and soldiers that are or shall be disabled by fight or other accidents in the service of the Crown, are to be provided for in the Royal Hospital at Chelsea, and in the meantime are to receive the allowances out of the money appointed for the use of the said Hospital. Which daily allowances and future provisions in Chelsea Hospital are also to be made to such non-commissioned officers and soldiers as having the Crown for 20 years'

In order to obtain a pension, a soldier would have to attend a Board at the Royal Hospital where his service would be checked and reviewed. A successful applicant would be issued with a parchment certificate noting his Service rank, regiment and a brief physical description. This certificate would then be presented to a Magistrate and an oath taken that he was the person in the document. Someone impersonating a Chelsea Pensioner could be sentenced to death or sent to the Colonies.

To be eligible for admission as an In-Pensioner today, a candidate must be:-

* In receipt of a Service or Disability Pension awarded for Army Service (or the Victoria Cross or George Cross annuity awarded in respect of bravery while serving in the British Army) and be of good character

* Normally at least 65 years of age; exceptionally a candidate may be admitted earlier if through disability he cannot earn his own living and received a pension for an Army disability

* Free from the obligation to support a wife or children

Each application is judged upon its merits.

Female Pensioners

Although no woman has ever been admitted to the Royal Hospital as an In-Pensioner, a number have been registered as Out-Pensioners.

Christina Ross at the centre of a group of soldiers from the 2nd Dragoons (Royal Scots Greys).

Christina Davis, alias Christopher Welsh, and also known as Mother Ross was awarded a pension of five pence a day in 1717. She had served in Flanders with the North British Dragoons and been badly wounded at the Battle of Ramillies in 1706. She was again wounded whilst serving with the Enniskillen Dragoons in Ireland. Her life story was written by Daniel Defoe and she died in 1739, aged 72.

Hannah Snell (1723-1792) was awarded a pension in 1750, having petitioned the Duke of Cumberland on her return from service with the Marines in India. She joined up in 1745 and was sent to India where she was wounded at the Siege of Pondicherry in 1748. She managed to keep the identity of her sex undetected throughout the four and a half years she was a soldier. On returning to England she sold her story to a publisher and became a celebrity on the London stage. She later ran a public house called 'The Widow in Masquerade' and died in 1792 in the lunatic asylum, Bedlam.

The Commissioners of the Royal Hospital decided in 1999 that, in principle, those female ex-soldiers who meet the eligibility rules of the Royal Hospital should be able to apply for entry, but only when suitable accommodation has been identified and prepared. It was further decided that a quorum of at least six females must be achieved before entry can start.

RUNNING THE HOSPITAL

The first three Commissioners (Wren, Fox and Ranelagh) were appointed in March 1692 to oversee and manage the Royal Hospital's affairs and to manage the pensions system.

Letters Patent in 1702/3 created an independent Board of five members. Originally all the Commissioners were appointed by name, but now eight hold their appointments by virtue of their office (three Government ministers, the Governor and Lieutenant Governor and three serving officers or officials from the Ministry of Defence). There are also up to ten 'Specially Appointed' Commissioners, who are distinguished individuals selected because of their experience and expertise in areas relevant to the Royal Hospital's work. These members serve for up to six years. The Board of Commissioners meets quarterly in the Council Chamber.

The history of the early funding of the Royal Hospital is set out above. Deductions from army pay, with occasional funding from other sources (such as the sale of commissions) continued to be the Royal Hospital's main source of revenue until 1847. Since then it has been supported by Government 'Grant-in-Aid'. This is supplemented by a small income derived from legacies, donations and the Army Prize Fund. The last element comes from shares of money allocated as the prize money for *battles and campaigns* in the 19th Century. Those that were unclaimed went to the Royal Hospital.

The great battles are listed on the walls of The Great Hall

HOSPITAL ADMINISTRATION

The internal administration of the Royal Hospital has always been organised on semi-military lines, with a Governor and other officers. Originally there were eight companies formed from the Foot and Dragoons, and a ninth from the Horse.

The In-Pensioners were armed, although only two barrels of powder were allowed to be held. The level of crime on the Westminster and Chelsea area was such that between 1715-1805, an armed patrol was maintained by night on the road from the Royal Hospital to St. James's. One In-Pensioner is known to have been killed undertaking this duty.

Over the decades a number of small changes have been made to the composition of the Royal Hospital, but the ethos remains essentially the same. Today the Governor is supported by the Lieutenant-Governor, the Secretary and nine Heads of Departments. Senior staff are mainly former regular Army officers or civil servants.

There are currently just under 350 In-Pensioners. They are organised into six companies under the care of a Captain of Invalids. Each Company has a Company Sergeant-Major and a complement of NCO's drawn from the In-Pensioners to assist in its running. They are responsible for the day-to-day administration in the Long Wards.

Around 100 In-Pensioners work voluntarily as guides, chapel attendants, clerical and shop staff and museum attendants and help in many other ways. They make a considerable contribution to the running of the Royal Hospital.

DAILY LIFE

The first Commissioners were instructed to draw up detailed regulations for feeding and clothing. The specified rations ('diet') were generous and each In-Pensioner was granted 12oz meat a day (fish on Friday), two loaves of bread, a quarter pound of cheese, two quarts of beer and an unspecified quantity of oatmeal and vegetables. Fish was discontinued from the menu in 1749.

By the start of the 19th century In-Pensioners began to eat their meals in their Wards. Initially cooked food was collected from the kitchen. Later food was taken to be reheated and all vegetables were prepared in the Wards. Communal eating only recommenced after the Second World War and not all the In-Pensioners wanted the change. Today meals are served seven days a week in the Great Hall and include breakfast, lunch and high tea. Only those Pensioners in the Infirmary or those who are unable to climb the steps to the Great Hall, eat elsewhere.

'A Grand Day Out and About'

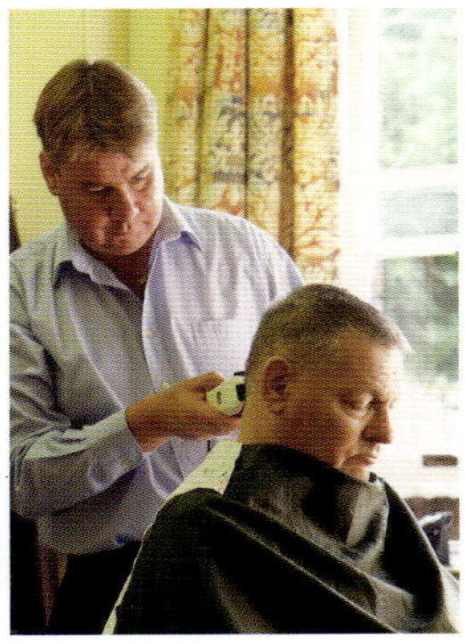

Daily Life: Getting measured up; Enjoying crafts and recreational pursuits; Having a trim
Bottom: An In-Pensioner's Berth
Main picture opposite: Looking out from The Long Wards

On arrival each new In-Pensioner is given a 'Berth' (bedroom) in a Long Ward and allocated to a Company. In certain circumstances entry may be directly into the Infirmary. The In-Pensioner surrenders his Army pension and in return receives board, lodging, clothing and full medical care.

In-Pensioners are given every opportunity to pursue a full active life within the Royal Hospital. In addition to undertaking voluntary jobs, In-Pensioners can enjoy many recreational pursuits including the use of a Club, the Prince of Wales Hall amenity centre, television and snooker rooms, a library, an arts and craft centre, a bowling green and allotment gardens.

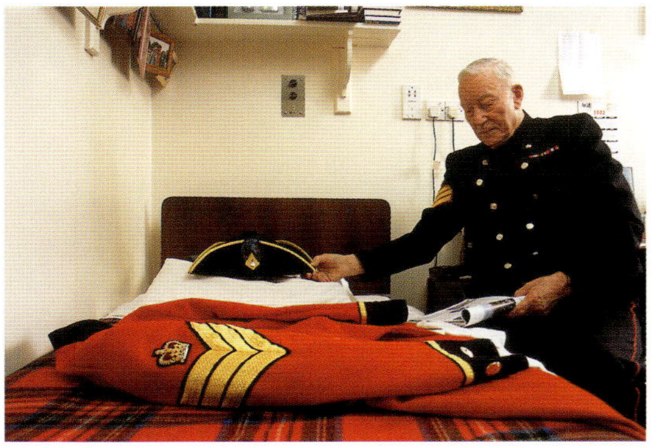

Trips are arranged regularly both within the United Kingdom and overseas, including Battlefield tours, sporting events and visits to military establishments. In 2002 a party went to the White House in Washington and met the President.

AUXIT JACO

Parades are now mainly limited to Annual Founder's Day, and the weekly Governor's Parade which takes place on Sunday morning before Chapel. The salute is taken by the Governor, Lieutenant Governor, Secretary or Adjutant with In-Pensioners from each Company on parade.

The Chapel plays an important part in the life of an In-Pensioner and visitors are always welcome to attend services.

Holidays and leave of absence is freely granted for up to six weeks at a time, although an In-Pensioner must be in residence during the week prior to Founder's Day for rehearsals, which take place in early June.

Within the confines of the Royal Hospital all In-Pensioners are encouraged to wear the Royal Hospital's informal uniform. They may wear civilian clothes if they wish. On all official occasions they wear the famous scarlet coats, completed at ceremonial events by tricorne hats. This dress is a modernised version of the uniform first introduced by the Duke of Marlborough, at the beginning of the 18th century.

Main picture opposite: An In-Pensioner enjoying the peace of The Chapel
This page (top): Founder's Day
This page (bottom): In the grounds of the Infirmary

THE INFIRMARY

The original Infirmary, built by Wren, comprised the existing South range in College Court. It provided accommodation for 35 patients and four nurses. This proved over the years to be inadequate, made worse during the Napoleonic Wars when the area over the Great Hall was used instead. In 1809, following complaints that the invalid In-Pensioners had to negotiate the 98 stairs to and from the Infirmary, Sir John Soane added to and converted Sir Robert Walpole's former house on the west side as an infirmary for 80 patients and staff.

This functioned until 1941, when the Infirmary was bombed, killing four nurses, the Wardmaster and eight In-Pensioners. The Infirmary patients were then evacuated to Ascott House (near Leighton Buzzard) from 1941-1946 and then to the Royal School for the Blind, at Leatherhead, from 1947-1960. The Soane Infirmary had been so seriously damaged it was considered to be beyond repair. The present Infirmary was built on the East side adjacent to the Chelsea Bridge Road using land formerly used by the Army Pensions Office. It was opened by HM The Queen Mother in 1961, with beds for 89 patients. It is to be rebuilt over the next few years.

CEREMONIES

FOUNDER'S DAY

The Royal Hospital Founder's Day is held on a day close to May 29th. This is the birthday of Charles II, as well as the date of his restoration as King in May 1660. It is also known as Oak Apple Day. The Parade is normally held during the first week of June when the Pensioners are usually reviewed by a member of the Royal Family. During the course of this celebratory day, the recently re-gilded statue of Charles II in Figure Court is decked in oak leaves and all participants in the Parade and spectators wear sprigs of oak leaves to commemorate the King's escape from the Parliamentary forces after the Battle of Worcester in 1651.

AND EVENTS

CAKE, CHEESE AND PUDDING

Every November, the Great Hall witnesses the ceremonial mixing of the Christmas Pudding. The In-Pensioners and staff are invited to assist with the stirring and in due course this gargantuan mixture is decanted into individual pudding basins and given to each In-Pensioner.

The Christmas festivities start in the Great Hall with the presentation of cheeses by the Dairy Council. During the sampling of the various varieties, a song known as the Quartermaster's Stores is sung:

There was cheese, cheese, wafting on the breeze,
In the Stores, in the Stores.
There was jam, jam, mixed up with the ham,
In the Quartermaster's Stores.

My eyes are dim I cannot see,
I have not brought my specs with me,
I have not brought my specs with me.........

Since 1950, the presentation of a Christmas cake and a bottle of ale to the In-Pensioners has been made by the Returned and Services League of Australia. Attended by members of the Australian High Commission and the Australian Defence Staff, the presentation takes place in the Great Hall with each Australian state taking it in turn to host the ceremony.

There was cheese, cheese, wafting on the breeze, In the Stores, in the Stores. There was jam, jam, mixed up with the ham, In the Quartermaster's Stores.

My eyes are dim I cannot see, I have not brought my specs with me, I have not brought my specs with me..

THE CHELSEA FLOWER SHOW

In 1913, the Board of Commissioners rented a portion of the Royal Hospital South Grounds, to the Royal Horticultural Society for their new annual show. Nearly a century later, the Chelsea Flower Show is visited by many thousands of people from all over the world and is the most prestigious Show in the horticultural calendar.

Held each May, it has been a great favourite of the Royal Family and a leading event in the London Season.

The building and dismantling of the showground takes about a month. One of the most remarkable features is the 'theme gardens' which seem to materialise virtually overnight from bare ground into the most elaborative and stunning exhibition gardens. An In-Pensioners' stall will always be found at the show stocking a wide range of gifts.

At other times of year the Royal Hospital grounds can be hired by organisations for public and trade events. The South Grounds also provide two football pitches and tennis courts for public use.

The Royal Hospital also maintains close links with the local community, playing its part in the Chelsea Festival and hosting events as part of London's 'String of Pearls'.

Main picture (above): The Chelsea Flower Show
Middle: The In-Pensioner's stall at the show
Right: The 'Theme Gardens'

In-Pensioners enjoy getting involved

and playing their part in the show…

Royalty

The Royal Hospital has always been proud to have a close link with the Sovereign. This continues strongly into the 21st century.

Her Majesty Queen Elizabeth II has reviewed the In-Pensioners on Founder's Day on four occasions. Reviewing officers have been members of the Royal family in every year since 1980.

The most significant Royal event in recent years occurred on 5th July 2002, when Her Majesty reviewed the Pensioners at Buckingham Palace and presented The Royal Hospital with its first 'colours' the Sovereign's Mace.

Queen Elizabeth II presents The Royal Hospital with its first 'colours', the Sovereign's Mace

Her Majesty Queen Elizabeth II presenting the Sovereign's Mace.

THE FUTURE

The Royal Hospital is now preparing itself to provide modern residential accommodation and care in its historic buildings yet maintaining the fabric of the buildings and traditions of the past. This will require:

* A new Infirmary
* Improved accommodation in the Long Wards and facilities for the In-Pensioners
* Improvements to the grounds to maintain the quality of life at the Royal Hospital and make it a pleasant place to live, work and visit.

The Royal Hospital Chelsea has provided a home to many of the Nation's old soldiers since 1692. Chelsea Pensioners are proud to continue a way of life and traditions established for over three hundred years. The Royal Hospital will continue to provide high quality residential care for old soldiers that have served their country loyally in both war and peace.

RH

HONI·SOIT·QUI·

HONI·SOIT·QUI·MAL·Y·PENSE

ROYAL HOSPITAL CHELSEA